Ladybird Readers

Forests

Series Editor: Sorrel Pitts
Written by Rachel Godfrey

LADYBIRD BOOKS

UK | USA | Canada | Ireland | Australia
India | New Zealand | South Africa

Ladybird Books is part of the Penguin Random House group of companies
whose addresses can be found at global.penguinrandomhouse.com.
www.penguin.co.uk   www.puffin.co.uk   www.ladybird.co.uk

Penguin
Random House
UK

First published 2018
001
Text copyright © Ladybird Books Ltd, 2018

All images copyright © BBC, 2006
Cover photograph by Tom Hugh-Jones copyright © BBC NHU, 2016
BBC and BBC Earth (word marks and logos) are trade marks of the
British Broadcasting Corporation and are used under licence.
BBC logo © BBC 1996. BBC Earth logo © 2014.

Printed in China

A CIP catalogue record for this book is available from the British Library

ISBN: 978–0–241–31958–1

All correspondence to:
Ladybird Books
Penguin Random House Children's
80 Strand, London WC2R 0RL

Ladybird Readers

BBC earth

Forests

Inspired by BBC Earth TV series and
developed with input from BBC Earth
natural history specialists

Contents

Picture words

forest

jungle

leaves

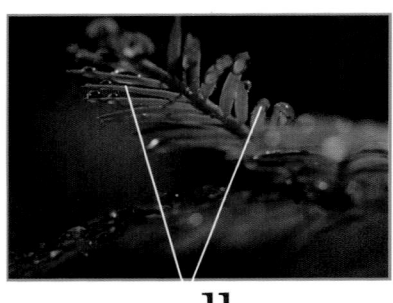

needles

mouse lemur

cicada

moth

insect

mandarin duck

duckling

bird of paradise

frog

Forests of the world

There have been forests on Earth for millions of years.

Three types of forests are:
temperate, tropical, and taiga.

Taiga forests

Temperate forests

Tropical forests

9

Types of forest

Temperate forests change temperature. Sometimes they are warm, and sometimes they are cold.

These animals live in temperate forests.

squirrel

Amur leopards

caterpillar

deer

capercaillies

Some tropical forests are called jungles. They are hot and wet.

Many different animals live in jungles.

elephant

frog

monkey

Taiga forests are cold for most of the year. Taiga forests go all around the Earth.

These animals live in taiga forests.

lynx

moose

Finding food in forests

It's difficult for animals to find food in the world's cold forests.

This is a taiga forest.

The conifer trees that grow in taiga forests have needles. Not many animals can eat them.

This moose is eating the needles of a conifer tree.

Some birds can open the pine cones of conifer trees with their beaks.

beak

pine cone

Lynx can travel hundreds of miles in the cold forest to find other animals to eat.

When forests are warm or hot, there are lots of leaves, flowers, fruit, eggs, and other animals to eat.

This monkey is eating flowers.

This squirrel
has found a
pine cone.

This bird has
some fruit.

Mouse lemurs

Mouse lemurs live in the forests in Madagascar. They eat at night.

These are baobab trees in Madagascar. When it rains, their leaves and flowers grow.

Mouse lemurs are about the same size as your hand.

mouse lemur

The baobab trees' flowers open very quickly at night. The flowers have nectar in them. This is a sweet drink for mouse lemurs and moths.

A moth drinks the nectar.

A mouse lemur drinks the nectar.

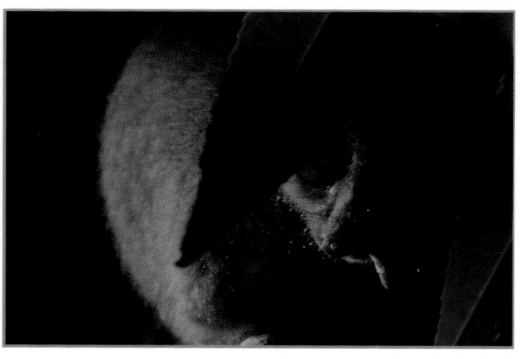

Then, the mouse lemur eats the moth.

Cicadas

It's a warm summer's evening in a temperate forest in North America. Millions of young cicadas come out from under the ground.

This is the biggest group of insects coming out from under the ground at one time on Earth. They have been under the ground for seventeen years.

First, the cicadas walk on the forest floor.

Then, they climb the trees.

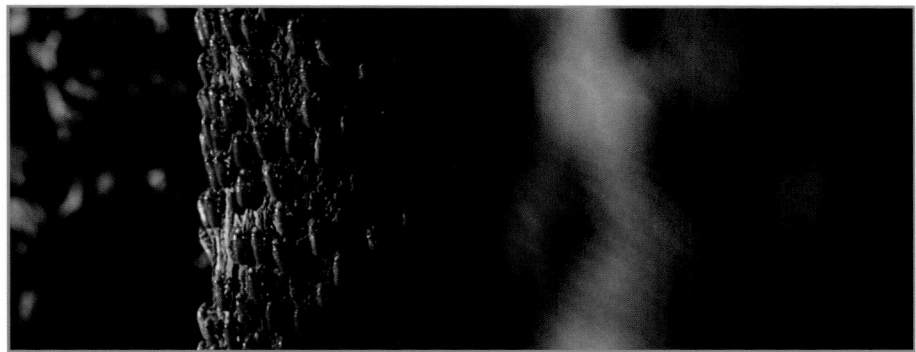

Finally, they turn into adults with wings.

Cicadas are not very good at flying with their new wings. Birds and other animals eat them.

The cicadas leave their eggs on trees. The babies hatch out of the eggs, and later they drop to the ground. The babies go under the ground.

Then, after a few days, the adult cicadas die. The animals of the forest must wait seventeen years for them to come again.

This cicada is leaving its eggs on a tree.

Mandarin ducks

Mandarin ducks live in the temperate forests of Europe and Russia.

The mother ducks lay their eggs high up in trees.

When the eggs have hatched,
the mother duck and her
ducklings leave the tree.
The mother jumps first.

A duckling looks out of the tree.

Then, her ducklings follow.

It's a long jump!

They fall to the forest floor.

Now, the mother duck and her ducklings must find water.

The mother duck and her ducklings aren't safe on the forest floor.

Finally, they get to a pool. Here, they are safe.

Birds of paradise

There are about forty different kinds of birds of paradise in the jungles of New Guinea. Each bird lives in a different part of the jungle.

Male birds of paradise use color, sound, and dance to make female birds look at them.

This is a male bird of paradise.
He has bright feathers.

This is a female bird of paradise.
She has brown feathers.

This bird sits high up in the trees. He opens his wings, and then he sings.

wings

This bird does a special dance on the forest floor.

This is the superb bird of paradise. First, the male bird makes a loud noise. He looks like a normal bird.

Then, he looks like this!

This female bird thinks he's interesting!

Jungle frogs

In the middle of the day,
the jungle is quiet. At night,
the jungle is noisy.

Male frogs wake up and call to the females. Each male frog wants to be the noisiest.

Different kinds of frogs make different noises.

The jungle is noisy, but the female frogs can only hear the calls of their own kind.

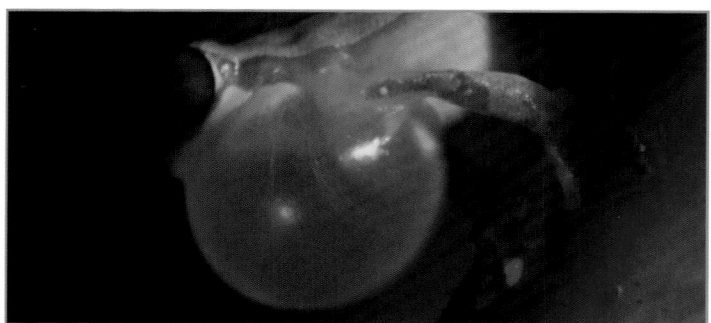

The gliding leaf frogs jump
from tree to tree in the jungle.
Their webbed feet help them
to travel slowly.

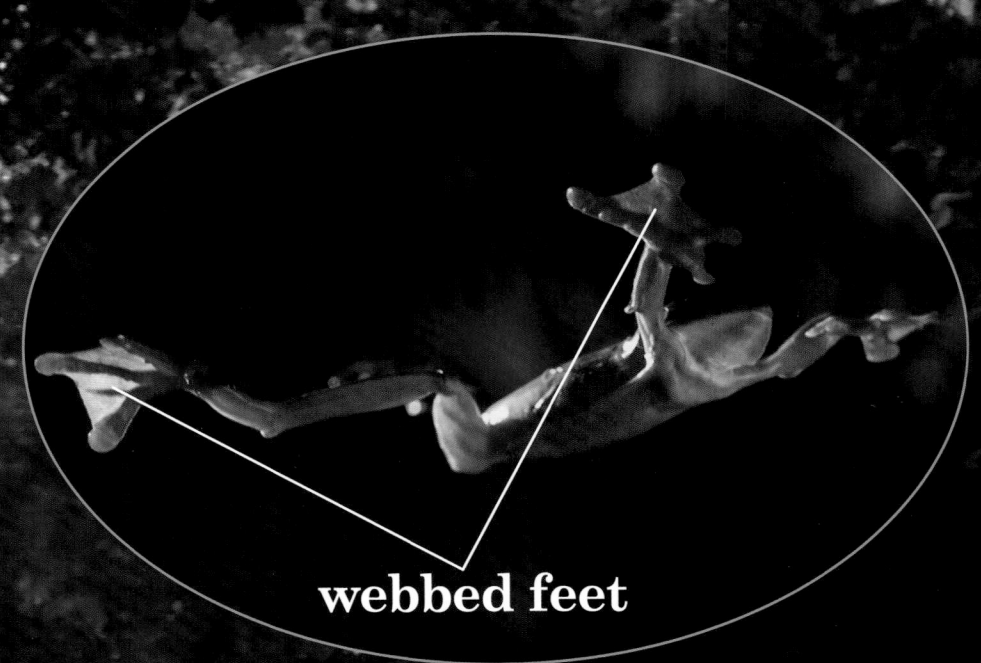

webbed feet

Forest elephants

Forest elephants live in West Africa. They are the biggest animals in the jungle.

They live in small groups in the dark forest, and often don't see other elephants for many weeks.

Sometimes, they must leave the trees and come into open spaces.

They join other groups
of elephants at the river.
There's a lot of mud here.

Other animals come to the mud, too.
Why? Below the mud, there's a
special kind of food.

The elephants are lucky.
They can use their long trunks
to get the food.

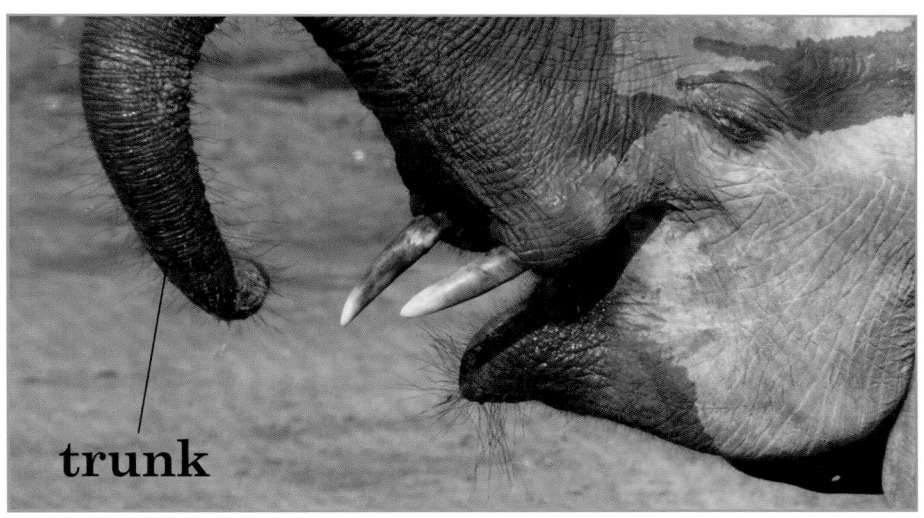

trunk

Problems for our forests

We are losing our forests and jungles, because people are cutting down trees. They make things with the wood. They burn the wood for cooking and keeping warm. They make open spaces for farm animals and to grow food.

Birds and animals need forests and jungles for homes and food.

Jungles cover only 3% of our planet, but more than half of the world's plants, insects, animals, and birds live here.

Our forests are important

We must look after our forests
to help the animals that live there.
People need forests, too.

We can help. We can plant
more trees. We can recycle more.

43

Activities

The key below describes the skills
practiced in each activity.

Spelling and writing

Reading

Speaking

Critical thinking

Preparation for the Cambridge
Young Learners exams

1 Match the words to the pictures.

1 forest

2 jungle

3 cicada

4 bird of paradise

a
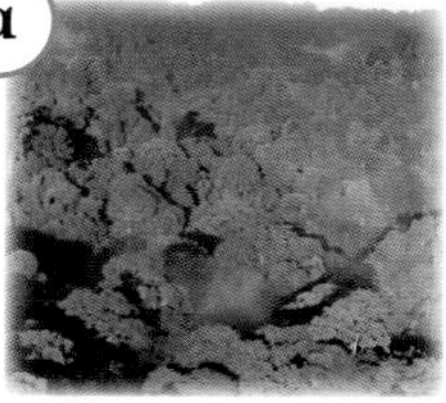

b
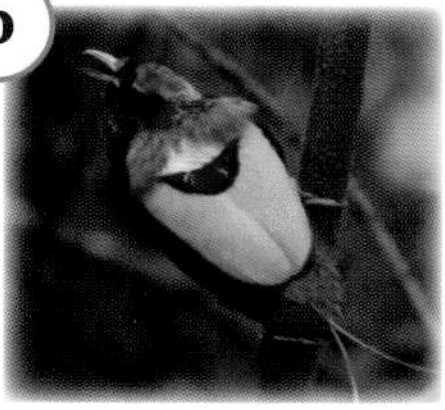

c
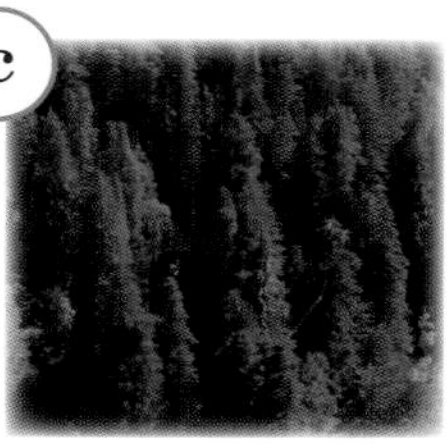

d
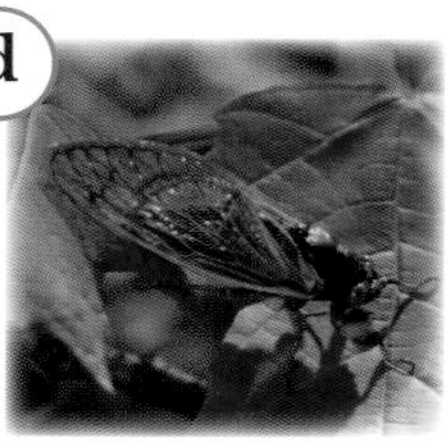

2 Look and read. Choose the correct words and write them on the lines.

lynx   forest   jungle   squirrel

1 This has been on Earth for millions of years.

forest

2 This kind of forest is hot and wet.

3 This animal lives in a temperate forest.

4 This animal lives in a taiga forest.

3 Circle the correct words.

1 Tropical forests are hot and **dry. / wet.**

2 Some **tropical / temperate** forests are called jungles.

3 Temperate forests change **time. / temperature.**

4 Sometimes temperate forests are warm, and sometimes they are **hot. / cold.**

5 Elephants live in hot **temperate / tropical** forests.

47

4 **Look and read.**
Write the answers.

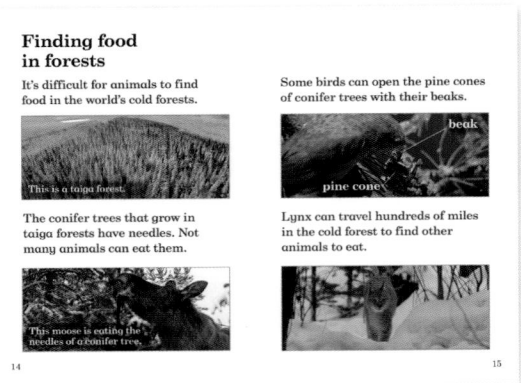

Finding food in forests

It's difficult for animals to find food in the world's cold forests.

This is a taiga forest.

The conifer trees that grow in taiga forests have needles. Not many animals can eat them.

This moose is eating the needles of a conifer tree.

Some birds can open the pine cones of conifer trees with their beaks.

beak

pine cone

Lynx can travel hundreds of miles in the cold forest to find other animals to eat.

14   15

1 What is this?

This is a taiga forest.

2 Which trees grow here?

....

3 Do these trees have leaves?

....

4 Which animal can eat
from these trees?

....

5 Look and read. Put a ✓ or a ✗ in the boxes. 📖 ✿ ❓

1 These are the needles of conifer trees. ✓

2 This bird has a strong beak. ☐

3 This monkey is eating a squirrel. ☐

4 This bird has some fruit. ☐

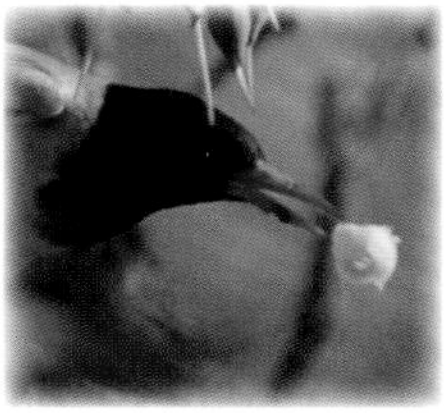

6 **Look at the letters.**
Write the words. 📖 ✏️ ✿

1 (e s u r m l)

Mouse ____lemurs____ live in
the forests in Madagascar.

2 (o b a b b a)

There are _____ trees
in the forests.

3 (e n t r a c)

The baobab trees' flowers
have _____ in them.

4 (k d i r n)

Moths and mouse lemurs
_____ the nectar.

5 (t s h m o)

Mouse lemurs eat the _____.

7 **Order the sentences. Write 1—5.**

.... The cicadas turn into adults with wings.

.... Young cicadas come out from under the ground and up into the forest.

.... The cicadas walk on the forest floor.

....1.... It's a warm summer's evening in a North American forest.

.... The cicadas climb the trees.

8 Read the sentences. Choose the correct words and write them on the lines. 📖 ✏️ ⬡

1 biggest	big	bigger
2 fly	to fly	flying
3 leave	left	leaving
4 dropping	dropped	drop

Cicadas are the [1] ___biggest___ group of insects who come out from under the ground at one time on Earth. They are not very good at [2] _____. They [3] _____ their eggs on trees. When the babies come out, they [4] _____ to the ground.

9 Write *yes* or *no*.

1 Mandarin ducks live
in tropical forests.   no

2 The mother ducks lay
their eggs in trees.

3 The mother and ducklings
must leave the tree.

4 The ducklings jump first.

5 It is a long jump, and they
fall to the forest floor.

6 Now, the mother and
ducklings must find
other ducks.

10 Talk to a friend. Ask and answer the questions about mandarin ducks. 💬 ❓

1

> *Where are these ducks?*

> *They are in a tree.*

2 Why does the mother lay her eggs in a tree, do you think?

3 Why must the mother and her ducklings leave the tree?

4 Why are the mother and her ducklings safe in the pool?

11 **Match the two parts of the sentences.**

1 Birds of paradise live in

2 The male bird of paradise

3 The female bird of paradise

4 The males want to make the

a has bright feathers.

b females look at them.

c the jungles in New Guinea.

d has brown feathers.

1 What is this bird called?

The superb bird of paradise.

2 What does the male superb bird of paradise do to make female birds look at him?

....

....

3 What does the female bird think about the male?

....

....

56

13 Circle the correct words.

1 In the day, the jungle is
noisy. / quiet.

2 At night, the jungle is
noisy. / quiet.

3 Male frogs call to the
babies. / females.

4 Each male frog wants to be
the **brightest. / noisiest.**

5 Different kinds of frog make
different / the same noises.

14 **Circle the correct pictures.**

1 This animal has webbed feet.

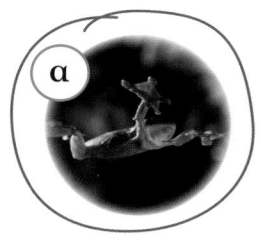  

2 This frog is jumping.

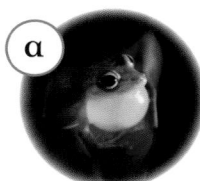 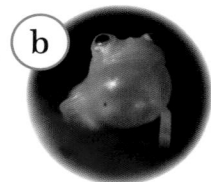 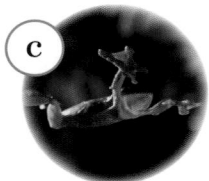

3 This frog is not calling
to female frogs.

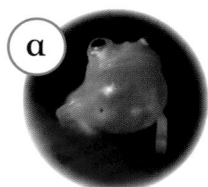 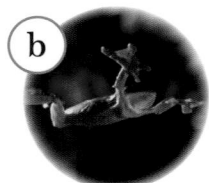 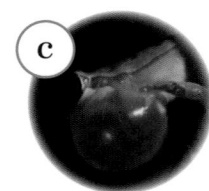

15 **Look and read. Write *yes* or *no*.**

1 Forest elephants are the biggest animals in the jungle. ....yes....

2 Forest elephants live in big groups. ....

3 They see lots of other elephants every day. ....

4 Forest elephants sometimes leave the trees. ....

5 They go to the river. ....

16 Talk to a friend about forest elephants.

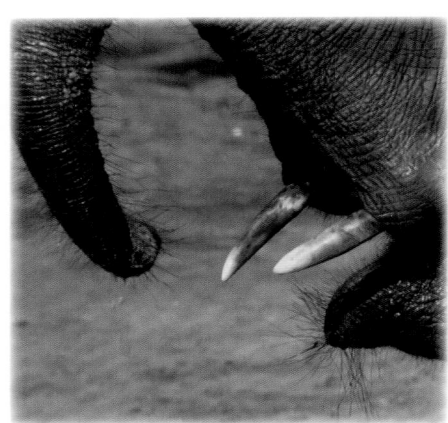

The forest elephants leave the trees, and come into open spaces.

17 **Write the sentences.**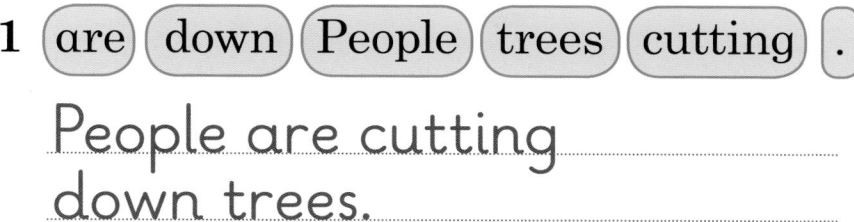

1 are   down   People   trees   cutting   .

People are cutting
down trees.

2 wood   burn   cooking   They   for   .

....

....

3 make   wood   People   with   things   .

....

....

18 Put a ✓ by all the animals in this book. 📖

1	mandarin ducks	✓	**2**	mouse lemurs	☐
3	tigers	☐	**4**	birds of paradise	☐
5	frogs	☐	**6**	sharks	☐
7	trees	☐	**8**	cicadas	☐
9	lions	☐	**10**	squirrels	☐
11	moths	☐	**12**	bears	☐

19 **Work with a friend to answer the questions about forests.** 💬

1 *Why are forests and jungles important?*

Birds and animals need them for homes and food.

2 How much of our planet do jungles cover?

3 Which things live in jungles?

4 What can we do to help?

Level 4

The Pied Piper of Hamelin

978-0-241-25378-6 ☐

The Wizard of Oz

978-0-241-25379-3 ☐

Sam and the Robots

978-0-241-25380-9 ☐

The Little Mermaid

978-0-241-29874-9 ☐

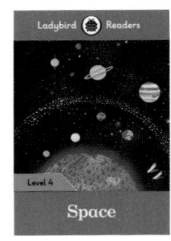

Space

978-0-241-25381-6 ☐

Pinocchio

978-0-241-28430-8 ☐

Alice in Wonderland

978-0-241-28431-5 ☐

Under the Oceans

978-0-241-29888-6 ☐

Knights and Castles

978-0-241-28432-2 ☐

Heidi

978-0-241-28433-9 ☐

Peter and the Wolf

978-0-241-28434-6 ☐

Dangerous Journeys

978-0-241-29891-6 ☐

A Fight with Underbite

978-0-241-29890-9 ☐

Sideswipe Loses his Head

978-0-241-29889-3 ☐

Aladdin

978-0-241-31606-1 ☐

Forests

978-0-241-31958-1 ☐

The Pony Games

978-0-241-31956-7 ☐